US MILITARY EQUIPMENT
AND VEHICLES

US ARMY
EQUIPMENT AND VEHICLES

BY DOUGLAS HUSTAD

CONTENT CONSULTANT
BILL ALLISON, PhD
PROFESSOR OF HISTORY
GEORGIA SOUTHERN UNIVERSITY

T0020667

Kids Core

An Imprint of Abdo Publishing
abdobooks.com

abdobooks.com

Published by Abdo Publishing, a division of ABDO, PO Box 398166, Minneapolis, Minnesota 55439. Copyright © 2022 by Abdo Consulting Group, Inc. International copyrights reserved in all countries. No part of this book may be reproduced in any form without written permission from the publisher. Kids Core™ is a trademark and logo of Abdo Publishing.

Printed in the United States of America, North Mankato, Minnesota
052021
092021

Cover Photo: Spc. Andrew McNeil/US Army/Defense Visual Information Distribution Service
Interior Photos: Staff Sgt. True Thao/US Army/Defense Visual Information Distribution Service, 4–5, 6, 28; Staff Sgt. Brian K. Ragin Jr./US Army/Defense Visual Information Distribution Service, 8; Sgt. Timothy Hamlin/US Army/Defense Visual Information Distribution Service, 10–11, 29 (top); Paolo Bovo/US Army/Defense Visual Information Distribution Service, 13; Sgt. Brendan Seiber/Defense Visual Information Distribution Service, 15; Sgt. 1st Class Chris Bridson/Defense Visual Information Distribution Service, 16; Capt. Brian Harris/Defense Visual Information Distribution Service, 18–19; Spc. Dana Clarke/US Army/Defense Visual Information Distribution Service, 20; Sgt. Nathan Franco/US Army/Defense Visual Information Distribution Service, 22; Pfc. Jordan Roy/US Army/Defense Visual Information Distribution Service, 23; Sgt. Trenton Lowery/US Army/Defense Visual Information Distribution Service, 25; Master Sgt. Michel Sauret/US Army Reserve/Defense Visual Information Distribution Service, 26; Spc. Jason Dangel/Defense Visual Information Distribution Service, 29 (bottom)

Editor: Katharine Hale
Series Designer: Jake Nordby

Library of Congress Control Number: 2020948455

Publisher's Cataloging-in-Publication Data

Names: Hustad, Douglas, author.
Title: US Army equipment and vehicles / by Douglas Hustad
Description: Minneapolis, Minnesota : Abdo Publishing, 2022 | Series: US military equipment and vehicles | Includes online resources and index.
Identifiers: ISBN 9781532195440 (lib. bdg.) | ISBN 9781644946176 (pbk.) | ISBN 9781098215750 (ebook)
Subjects: LCSH: Armies--Juvenile literature. | United States. Army--Transport service--Juvenile literature. | United States. Army--Equipment--Juvenile literature. | Vehicles, Military--Juvenile literature. | Military supplies--Juvenile literature. | Military paraphernalia--Juvenile literature.
Classification: DDC 623.7--dc23

CONTENTS

The US Army uses the M1 tank in training exercises around the world.

CHAPTER 1

UNSTOPPABLE

There is a low rumble in the distance. The sound gets louder. Suddenly, an M1 Abrams tank bursts over the top of a hill. Its long main **cannon** can take out almost anything in its path. Its smaller guns can handle other threats that pop up.

Built like a Tank

Machine gun

Main cannon

Turret

Hull

Track

The Abrams has a rotating turret that allows the main cannon to aim. The hull protects the soldiers inside.

Few things can stop an M1 and its four-person crew. The US Army's main battle tank can power through most conditions. Its tracked wheels mean it won't get stuck in mud or snow. It has been the army's top tank for more than 40 years.

The Abrams is a fitting symbol for the army. It can go almost anywhere on land at up to 30 miles per hour (50 km/h). And it has the firepower to win battles.

About the Army

The US Army is a branch of the US military. It is the largest and oldest branch. Its mission is to win America's wars by dominating on land.

M1s around the World

The M1 Abrams is the most common tank in the US Army's fleet. It is also in use by six other nations around the world. Approximately 10,000 M1s have been built since 1979.

Soldiers can name M1 Abrams tanks. The name is printed on the main cannon.

The army's vehicles are tools for soldiers to do their jobs. They carry troops from place to place. They protect troops as they fight. And they haul important supplies. Equipment such as weapons helps soldiers defend themselves.

The army engages in a wide range of missions around the world. All of its members do their best to keep their country safe. Vehicles like the M1 Abrams tank help them do just that.

Explore Online

Visit the website below. Does it give any new information about tanks that wasn't in Chapter One?

M1 Abrams Tank

abdocorelibrary.com/army
-equipment-vehicles

The M4 can be fired by a soldier standing, crouching, or lying on the ground.

CHAPTER 2

EQUIPMENT AND WEAPONS

The US Army has nearly 500,000 active soldiers. An army that size requires many different weapons for different uses. But there is one weapon given to every soldier. It is the M4 rifle.

The M4 has been the army's **standard issue** weapon since 2016. It is an improvement on old rifles. It is shorter. This makes it easier to handle in small spaces. The rifle is also lighter. It weighs less than 8 pounds (3.6 kg). It doesn't add as much weight to the heavy load soldiers already have to carry. The M4 is a selective-fire weapon. That means it can fire in different ways. It can fire a single shot with every pull of the trigger. Or it can fire a burst of three at once. The M4 can hit targets up to 1,970 feet (600 m) away.

Heavy Weapons

Some weapons take multiple soldiers to operate. These weapons have a longer range and can do more damage than a handheld gun.

Loaders, gunners, and spotters all have a role in operating an Mk 19.

The Mk 19 is a **grenade** launcher. It sits on a stand. Two or three people usually operate it.

One person fires the weapon. Another person feeds it a belt containing grenades.

It can fire up to one grenade every second. The grenades launch up to 2,419 yards (2,212 m). The grenades are powerful enough to damage nearby ground vehicles or aircraft.

Rocket Power

The army employs a few rocket launchers, such as the AT4. Soldiers carry the AT4 on

Meals on the Go

Soldiers aren't always near a kitchen. Meals Ready-to-Eat (MREs) allow soldiers to eat anywhere. MREs can be eaten hot or cold. They contain an entrée, side dish, and dessert. MREs come with a heater and utensils. They don't need refrigeration and can last more than three years.

The AT4 fires without recoil, meaning it does not jump backward from the force of firing.

their shoulders. It fires rockets at high speeds for a long distance.

The AT4 is a portable way to launch powerful weapons. It is very light at 16.5 pounds (7.5 kg). But it can hit targets nearly 1,000 feet (300 m) away. Weapons used at a distance help keep troops out of harm's way.

ENVG-Bs allow soldiers to use their weapons to see around corners.

Other Equipment

Weapons are not the only important equipment for soldiers. Night-vision goggles (NVGs) allow soldiers to see in the dark. In 2019, the army tested NVGs that could do even more. Enhanced Night Vision Goggle-Binoculars (ENVG-Bs) help soldiers see through smoke and dust. Soldiers wear ENVG-Bs on their helmets. These goggles connect to their mapping system. They help soldiers keep track of each other. The goggles also connect to the sight on a soldier's weapon. A soldier can point a weapon around a corner and see if enemy troops are there. The army began using ENVG-Bs in 2020.

Further Evidence

Look at the website below. Does it give any new evidence to support Chapter Two?

Army Weapons

abdocorelibrary.com/army
-equipment-vehicles

Humvees can handle driving through sand, deep water, and more.

CHAPTER 3

DOMINANCE ON LAND

The equipment troops use requires vehicles to haul it. One US Army land vehicle has finished more missions and driven more miles than any other. It's the high-mobility multipurpose wheeled vehicle (HMMWV). It is best known as the Humvee.

The hatch on top of some Humvees allows soldiers to keep watch.

The Humvee entered combat in 1989. Since then, hundreds of thousands more have entered service. The Humvee can carry troops and weapons over many kinds of **terrain**. It can cross deserts at speeds of 55 miles per hour (89 km/h). It can plow through rivers 2.5 feet (76 cm) deep. Humvees come in different body styles. Some have hatches on top. These allow troops to look out on patrol.

The Jeep

Before the Humvee, there was the jeep. The jeep began as an army transport vehicle in 1940. It was so popular with troops that the company started to make vehicles for **civilians**. Jeep is now part of the Chrysler company, one of the largest automakers in the world.

The JLTV will eventually replace the Humvee.

On August 25, 2015, the army announced it had selected the design for a new vehicle to replace the Humvee. The Joint Light Tactical Vehicle (JLTV) features more **armor** than the Humvee while performing the same duties. But the Humvee was planned to remain in service alongside the JLTV until at least 2050.

Fighting Vehicles

The M1 Abrams is the army's main tank. But the army has many fighting vehicles. The M2 and

The M2, *pictured*, and M3 are not called tanks because their main cannons are too small.

M3 fighting vehicles do not lead battles like the Abrams does. But they carry troops and smaller weapons to help support a battle. Troops can fire weapons from inside the vehicle to stay protected.

The M113 is an armored **personnel** carrier. It transports troops and supplies into battle in total safety. The M113 is one of the most heavily used armored vehicles.

Armored Trucks

The wars in Iraq and Afghanistan brought a new threat to American troops. Improvised explosive devices (IEDs) were small homemade bombs that were hard to detect. They could go off any time a military vehicle rolled by.

Trucks such as the M1117 Guardian were designed to protect troops from IEDs. The Guardian carries an Mk 19 grenade launcher and other weapons. But its armor is its main protection. The thick plates block most blasts.

Army combat medics use the M113 to provide medical care in battle.

Mechanics play an important role in keeping vehicles such as the M1117 ready for battle.

It also has tires designed to not go flat. And it has a system that cleans the air to protect troops from a chemical attack.

The US Army has a wide range of missions. Its vehicles and equipment are just as varied. They all help the army do its job to keep Americans safe.

In 2014, Samantha Brumley became the first female M1 Abrams tank mechanic in the Oregon Army National Guard. Brumley said:

> I'm proud of being the first female tank mechanic, but I don't like getting called out on it because it's different. . . . It's just a job and an opportunity. . . . I wouldn't trade it.

Source: Kevin Hartman. "Face of Defense: Female Tank Mechanic Likes Dirty Work." *US Department of Defense*, 26 Aug. 2014, defense.gov. Accessed 6 May 2020.

What's the Big Idea?

What is this quote's main idea? Explain how the main idea is supported by details.

IMPORTANT GEAR

M1 Abrams Tank

- Tracked, armored vehicle

- Can travel up to 30 miles per hour (50 km/h) off road

- Can carry four crew members

M4 Rifle

- Selective fire weapon
- Weighs less than 8 pounds (3.6 kg)
- Range of 1,970 feet (600 m)

HMMWV (Humvee)

- Armed troop transport vehicle
- Can reach speeds of 55 miles per hour (89 km/h) fully loaded
- Can drive through water 2.5 feet (76 cm) deep

Glossary

armor
extra protection, often made of thick metal, surrounding something.

cannon
a type of large gun that fires long distances

civilians
people who are not in the military

grenade
a weapon that explodes after being thrown or launched

personnel
the people who make up an organization

standard issue
equipment that is commonly assigned to people

terrain
the surface of land or ground and its features

Online Resources

To learn more about US Army equipment and vehicles, visit our free resource websites below.

Visit **abdocorelibrary.com** or scan this QR code for free Common Core resources for teachers and students, including vetted activities, multimedia, and booklinks, for deeper subject comprehension.

Visit **abdobooklinks.com** or scan this QR code for free additional online weblinks for further learning. These links are routinely monitored and updated to provide the most current information available.

Learn More

Abdo, Kenny. *United States Army*. Abdo Publishing, 2019.

Bassier, Emma. *Military Vehicles*. Abdo Publishing, 2020.

London, Martha. *Military Weapons*. Abdo Publishing, 2020.

Index

About the Author

Douglas Hustad is a freelance author primarily of science and history books for young people. He, his wife, and their dogs live in the northern suburbs of San Diego, California.